Garden Style: A Beginner's Guide to 25 Garden Styles

Gardening Basics for Beginners Series

Nina Greene

This book is dedicated to anyone researching garden ideas, styles and designs.

Copyright © 2014 by Speedy Publishing LLC

All rights reserved. No part of this publication may be reproduced, distributed or transmitted in any form or by any means, including photocopying, recording, or other electronic or mechanical methods, without the prior written permission of the publisher, except in the case of brief quotations embodied in critical reviews and certain other noncommercial uses permitted by copyright law. For permission requests, write to the publisher, addressed "Attention: Permissions Coordinator," at the address below.

Speedy Publishing LLC (c) 2014
40 E. Main St., #1156
Newark, DE 19711
www.speedypublishing.co

Ordering Information:
Quantity sales; Special discounts are available on quantity purchases by corporations, associations, and others. For details, contact the "Special Sales Department" at the address above.

-- 1st edition

Manufactured in the United States of America

Table of Contents

Publisher's Notes i

Introduction ii

Chapter 1: Butterfly Garden 1

Chapter 2: Container Garden 3

Chapter 3: Contemporary Garden 5

Chapter 4: English Garden 7

Chapter 5: Formal Garden 9

Chapter 6: Herb Garden 11

Chapter 7: Informal Garden 13

Chapter 8: Italian Garden 15

Chapter 9: Meadow Garden 17

Chapter 10: Meditation Garden 19

Chapter 11: Mediterranean Garden 21

Chapter 12: Organic Garden 23

Chapter 13: Prairie Garden 25

Chapter 14: Raised Bed Garden 27

Chapter 15: Rock Garden 29

Chapter 16: Rose Garden 31

Chapter 17: Southwest Garden 33

Chapter 18: Theme Garden 35

Chapter 19: Tropical Garden 37

Chapter 20: Tuscan Garden 39

Chapter 21: Vegetable Garden 41

Chapter 22: Vertical Garden 43

Chapter 23: Water Garden 45

Chapter 24: Woodland Garden 47

Chapter 25: Zen Garden 49

Chapter 26: Final Considerations In Selecting A Garden Style 51

Meet the Author 53

More Books by Nina Greene 54

Publisher's Notes

Disclaimer

This publication is intended to provide helpful and informative material. It is not intended to diagnose, treat, cure, or prevent any health problem or condition, nor is intended to replace the advice of a physician. No action should be taken solely on the contents of this book. Always consult your physician or qualified health-care professional on any matters regarding your health and before adopting any suggestions in this book or drawing inferences from it.

The author and publisher specifically disclaim all responsibility for any liability, loss or risk, personal or otherwise, which is incurred as a consequence, directly or indirectly, from the use or application of any contents of this book.

Any and all product names referenced within this book are the trademarks of their respective owners. None of these owners have sponsored, authorized, endorsed, or approved this book.

Always read all information provided by the manufacturers' product labels before using their products. The author and publisher are not responsible for claims made by manufacturers.

Print Edition 2014

Introduction

Ask 10 people what a garden is and you are apt to get 10 different answers. Every garden style is open to interpretation and there is no "black and white" definition for any one style. Even the same garden style may have different meanings and variations in different parts of the world.

Every single garden style or design would be impossible to put into one book. The goal of this book, Introduction to 25 Garden Styles, is to give new gardeners a basic and general overview on some common and popular garden styles.

Take a look at the different garden styles and I hope you become inspired to create something uniquely wonderful in your own space.

CHAPTER 1: BUTTERFLY GARDEN

A butterfly garden is a type of wildlife garden that has an environment that invites butterflies and moths to frequent and is also conducive for procreation.

People create butterfly gardens to enjoy these fascinating, beautiful and colorful creatures as a hobby or for simple leisurely enjoyment. Creating a butterfly garden, regardless of the reason, helps the butterfly species grow as there has been a decrease in their population due to the destruction of their natural habitats.

Butterflies do not feed on typical garden plants. You will need to research the type of plants butterflies like and determine what will grow well in your climate. It is also a good idea to research the different types of butterflies and which ones are common in your location. This step will assist you with plant selections.

Plants that attract butterflies include sunflowers, yellow cone flowers, purple cone flowers, marigolds, salvias, poppies, certain types of lilies, cosmos, asters, daisies, coreopsis, milkweed, verbenas, zinnias, and buddleia (otherwise known as butterfly bush) just to name a few.

Plants and flowers are not the only way to attract butterflies. Install butterfly houses, water, shelter for harsh weather, shade for hot weather, sand for where they can puddle, rocks where they can warm themselves and other resources that support their ideal environment.

CHAPTER 2: CONTAINER GARDEN

Container gardening is a technique that allows you to enjoy the beauty of nature by growing plants, flowers, fruits, vegetables and herbs. Any container that can hold a good amount of soil, the weight of the growing plants, and has good drainage holes is fit for container gardening.

Container gardening is ideal for limited spaces, enhancing interiors, decks and patios but is not limited to enclosed and covered areas. Hanging baskets, planter boxes, large flowerpots and wooden barrels are just a few examples of commonly used containers.

Not all containers are suitable for container gardening. There are certain needs and specifications you need to be familiar with before you purchase a container.

Make sure the container you purchase has a wide opening. A container with a narrow opening hinders the growth of the plant outwards that might result for it to grow inwards and thereby break your container in the long run.

GARDEN STYLES

Do not use cheap plastic pots and terracotta pots. Cheap plastic pots deteriorate with UV rays from the sun. Terracotta pots are porous and dry easily thereby drying your plants as well.

Glazed ceramic pots with proper drainage holes (1/2 inch across) is one of the best options for container gardening. If you live in a warmer part of the world, choose a ceramic pot with a light color so it will not absorb as much heat.

Wood containers can be built to fit a specific location but are susceptible to rot. Redwood and cedar containers are rot resistant and can be used without treating or staining. Avoid wood containers treated with creosote, penta or any other toxic chemicals.

The number of plants and their size will determine the size of the container you need. Small pots dry out quicker and also restrict the root area. Containers that hold between 15 and 120 quarts are recommended.

Hanging baskets need to be lined with sphagnum moss for water retention and need to be kept out of the afternoon sun.

Container gardening is practical, aesthetically pleasing and only limited by a gardener's imagination.

Chapter 3: Contemporary Garden

A contemporary garden is a style designed to look elegant, smart and classy. By combining certain elements together you can make your garden emulate a contemporary style. A contemporary style garden is a garden that has a simple and minimalistic design, and one with symmetrical and balanced elements. This style of garden works best if you have a modern house or a country town house since both designs are classy and simple in nature.

Contemporary garden style works toward hard landscaping, structure and design more than the actual plants themselves. Hard landscaping is the most important aspect of a contemporary garden. Some of the elements and features you should look for in materials that you need to decorate your garden are as follows; Look for items that have clean lines meaning a smooth and seamless design with smooth textures. Specific items would be furniture or materials made from slate, polished stone, concrete, wood, glass, plastics as these materials offer a smooth finish. You can still express a bit of your creativity with small and little details such as flowerpots, but do not go overboard. Finally, use flowers sparingly or better yet, use just one species and keep the greenery lush and rich to make your garden clean and simple.

Chapter 4: English Garden

Mention an English garden and common images that come to mind are thatched roof cottages, colorful flowers, maybe a rose garden or neatly trimmed boxwood hedges. English gardens evoke a natural feel and are meant to look as though no planning went into creating their charm, tranquility and beauty.

The English garden originated in England during the early 18th century and quickly spread across Europe. There is no need to travel to the English countryside to experience an English garden. These gardens are versatile and can thrive in any landscape setting including the cold, northern parts of the United States.

Below are some suggestions of plants and design elements commonly found in English gardens:

Popular flowers that are grown in an English garden are perennial plants such as bee balm, daffodils, foxglove, hibiscus, hydrangea, and veronica. Do not forget roses as no English garden would be complete without them. Try to include a variety of heights and bloom times in order to have something blooming from early spring through late autumn. To compliment perennial plants add annual flowers such as cosmos, marigolds and pansies.

English gardens need some structure; borders or walls will accomplish this. Borders should be colorful, can be curvy, and narrow at some parts while deeper in others. Walls create privacy and definition to your garden. Choose a hard material such as wood or brick, or add a living hedge from privet, boxwood or yews.

Do not overlook the importance of structures and accessories to add variety and appeal to your garden. Entry gates, arbors, pergolas and trellis can be blended or softened with climbing roses, ivy or wisteria. Accessory items can include benches, garden furniture, fountains, statues, antique watering cans and rusty wagon wheels.

Lastly, walking paths are a nice feature if your garden is large. Grass paths create a soft appearance and are soft to walk on. Flagstones, bricks or pavers will give a classic look and reduce maintenance.

Chapter 5: Formal Garden

A formal garden is defined by geometrical shapes through the use of plants that can be trained as hedges. Formal gardens are commonly associated with the renaissance era and garden mazes are also commonly found in courtyards of castles and old elegant buildings, especially in English countries.

If you are thinking of creating a formal garden there are a few things to consider. The most beautiful formal gardens require large amounts of land since the beauty and artistry of a formal garden is a feature not with the kinds of plants in the garden but primarily the patterns created by your gardens floor imprint.

Some plants or hedges commonly used in formal gardens are sensitive to climate. Some parts of the world may not be able to execute formal gardens that are found in areas like Europe and the United States. The beauty of a formal garden is in its geometrical patterns which require constant tending. It is important to keep hedges trimmed to maintain your desired shape and height, as an untended hedge can grow wildly and look unappealing.

GARDEN STYLES

A formal garden can be executed in your own backyard without a large expanse of land. The key to a formal garden in small spaces is planning your layout. In some cases where hedging is difficult to achieve, the geometric patterns can still be achieved through the use of wall climbing plants. This is particularly useful for spaces which are bound by walls. In some situations bricks and concrete can be used to create the borders of the geometric patterns in place of actual hedging to achieve the same look and feel. Although formal gardens have a rather traditional implication, your design should not be limited by these concepts. Utilize the basic concepts of a formal garden and then add your own twist by adding unconventional plants not commonly seen in formal gardens.

CHAPTER 6: HERB GARDEN

Herbs have been around and in use since prehistoric times. Herbs have been used throughout the ages for food seasoning, the preservation of meat, religion, tanning and dying leather, politics, superstition, masking odors, health, and romance. Today, herbs are most commonly used in Traditional Chinese Medicine and for flavoring in our foods.

If you are thinking about starting an herb garden the good news is that deciding what you want to grow should be easy. Grow herbs that you love and already use on a regular basis. Herb gardeners that enjoy cooking often have gardens that contain the top ten cooking herbs; dill, basil, rosemary, chives, sage, mint, cilantro, oregano, parsley, and thyme.

An herb garden is actually like other gardens in format and maintenance but only with herbs as its primary plants. Herbs are versatile and can be grown in dozens of ways. Herb gardens can be can be used as groundcover, trimmed into hedges, be part of a larger vegetable garden or simply planted in a separate space exclusive for growing spices.

Herbs flourish in pots and can also be grown in window boxes, baskets and raised beds. Herbs require daily direct sunlight and adequate soil that drains well.

Several of the most popular herbs, such as Chives, Mint, Parsley, and Sage are very easy to grow. Just be aware that Mint and Sage will take over your garden if you allow it to.

Chapter 7: Informal Garden

The most important goal of an informal garden is to create a naturalistic atmosphere. Informal gardens are unbalanced, asymmetrical and do not follow regular lines and patterns. They are casual, laidback and create a homey and relaxed atmosphere that can easily be incorporated into the design of various house styles such as rustic homes and craftsman-style bungalows.

Without even realizing it, you might already have an informal garden in your own backyard. Today's informal garden can be filled with plants such as herbs, vegetables, perennial flowers, wildflowers, fruit trees, and annuals. Just about anything can be planted and added to this garden design for practical purposes or just for beauty.

If you are in the planning stage of designing (or adding to) your own informal garden consider the following tips to make your garden look more appealing.

GARDEN STYLES

<u>Curves</u> - Create your lines with gentle curves.

<u>Balance</u> - Plants as well as their structure or volume should be equal to the opposite side.

<u>Scale</u> - Grow plants that complement the size of your house or space.

<u>Illusion</u> - Put large plants in front and smaller plants in the back to make your garden appear bigger.

CHAPTER 8: ITALIAN GARDEN

Italy is well known for good fruits, good vegetables, and some of the most beautiful gardens. Italian gardens are made to serve the purpose of admiration for nature's beauty and relaxation.

One essential component in an Italian garden is shaded space to sit, relax, and enjoy a nice conversation over tea with friends or simply to take in the beauty of nature. An Italian garden should have a fountain or water running in a small stream placed in the heart of the garden and creeping vines like strawberries or other scented plants. To add beauty, evergreens or hedges can be planted and trimmed to form spectacular designs. Herbs and other plants can be placed in pots and placed symmetrically on a patio. To complete the look of elegance, marble flooring for the patio or reclaimed bricks for the pathway of the garden will do the trick.

Italian gardening is an art and an understanding of how nature works. It presents grandeur but teaches humility. Italians have suffered over the course of time and they learned to grow their own crops, in their own backyards, for consumption. The theme of

GARDEN STYLES

an Italian garden should be about elegance, beauty and perseverance.

Chapter 9: Meadow Garden

The intention of a meadow garden should be to recreate the impression of wide acres of grassy land sprawling with wildflowers found in natural meadows. These natural meadows are maintained through several environmental factors that allow the diversity of plants to thrive without turning into woodlands. There are coastal meadows dictated by the elements of the sea and desert meadows which are home to species suited for low precipitation. The richness and abundance of plants coexisting with each other is the same desired effect for a meadow garden.

Although this garden theme seems easy and requires low maintenance, creating the look of a natural meadow can involve a lot of time and effort. Grasses and wildflowers are the essential plants for creating this kind of garden. However, finding the right species that will grow in a certain areas can be challenging. This is usually determined by surveying the soil, the climate and precipitation level in the areas. The right plants for this kind of garden are those that will naturally blend with each other after some time. An ideal meadow garden has a variety of perennials, annuals and biennials so there is a continuous provision of color for the garden.

Meadows comprise mostly of grass, like muhly grass, Indian grass, fountain grass, feather reed grass, buffalo grass and sheep fescue. Aside from decorative reasons, grasses serve a variety of functions. These include providing protection and support for tall flowers, preventing soil erosion, adding color and texture to the landscape and filling spaces around flowers that might be occupied by weeds. Removing weeds is one of the major difficulties for this type of garden, especially for larger patches of land. For small meadows weed problems are more manageable.

Other plants typically found in this garden are coreopsis, black-eyed Susan, goldenrods, blazing star and butterfly weed. Different combinations for grasses and wildflowers can be used to achieve that wild diversity found in a natural meadow. Some meadow landscapes even include pathways made of brick and gravel. Keep in mind that the soil and seeding is crucial when starting a meadow garden but once the plants have settled in, long term maintenance is reduced.

CHAPTER 10: MEDITATION GARDEN

Any beautifully designed garden can provide a trance-like effect on people, but what really defines a genuine place for personal meditation?

A meditation garden should provide a haven for relaxation and peace. It is a place where the stress of life can be momentarily forgotten and where drained energy can be revived. It should clear the mind of negative thoughts and align it to a positively focused perception.

The design of a meditation garden should be considered very carefully by the owner. It is advisable to take note of objects, materials, environment, and colors that make the owner's mind relax comfortably. Personal preferences are very important, more important than the garden theme. For example, a healthy mix of Asian and Western designs can work as long as it is beneficial to the owner's peace of mind.

Basic things to consider when designing a meditation garden:

- Size of the garden
- Views from the garden
- Acoustics of the garden
- Terrain

The size of a meditation garden should conform to the owner's budget. Getting stressed over financing a meditation garden might affect the owner's impression of the finished project. There should be adequate division of areas for trees, ponds, fountains, ornamental plants, pergolas, trellises, or gazebos. If the owner doesn't live alone, assign fences or entrances that allow privacy to specific parts of the garden.

There must be a view in the meditation garden that can immediately catch the attention of anyone who enters it. It can be a group of cleverly placed shrubs and flowering plants, a majestic tree, the sunrise or sunset, the beach, etc. There should be a focal point; the owner's most favorite spot.

The garden's terrain also provides visual pleasure and inspiration. Should there be slopes? Where should grass be placed and where should soil be changed? Consulting pictures of popular gardens can give the owner an idea of the best terrain shape.

Trees, green walls, and fences can block out unnecessary noise inside the garden. Professional garden designers can analyze the location first and provide useful suggestions to keep the garden as quiet as possible.

Chapter 11: Mediterranean Garden

Mediterranean garden designs revolve around light, warmth, simplicity, relaxation and the laidback outdoor living associated with the Mediterranean. Inspired from the gardens of Italy, Spain, Greece and Southern France, this traditional garden design uses earthy and natural materials like stone, gravel and terracotta to create the landscape. This type of garden is ideal for warmer climates, but with the right plants and arrangement, it is still possible to capture the warm and bright feel of the Mediterranean even in a colder environment.

Creating a relaxing outdoor space is essential to this garden concept so it is typical to find benches, chairs and tables for this set-up. Cushions are added as decorations for that hint of color. A water element is should be included when creating a Mediterranean garden. A shade of blue can be used in ceramic tiles and furniture and sandstone is used to get a sun-bleached effect.

The ideal plants for a Mediterranean garden include those that can withstand the heat of the summer and have little tolerance to frost. The Mediterranean is also known for its variety of herbs, so some gardens have perennial herbs like rosemary, thyme and oregano. Rosemary, with its aroma and deep green foliage is also used to make clipped topiary that is common in Mediterranean gardens. Lavender and jasmine are some of essential plants used to add a bit of scent. The typical trees found in this garden are olive, palm and oleanders, while Italian cypress can give height to the design. The colors of the garden not only come from the furniture and the stone tiles, but from the plants as well so terracotta pots are used to plant flowers like geraniums and santolina.

CHAPTER 12: ORGANIC GARDEN

Organic gardening is a method that grows food in a healthy, sustainable way that does not harm the environment. Organic gardening is chemical-free gardening relying on no synthetic products like fertilizers and pesticides.

What does a gardener need to do to make a garden organic? Use organic matter such as animal waste, dried grass clippings and kitchen scraps as soil amendment. Plant crops in wide spaces; if they are planted too closely to each other fungal diseases can run rampant. Water plants in the morning as water in the afternoon or evening attracts diseases. Also be diverse with crops; a mix of plants will ensure that an infestation will not wipe out everything in the garden.

Crop rotation is a surefire way to ensure that diseases will not breed in your garden. Not all insects found in the garden are harmful; some of them can be beneficial and are a natural solution to pest control without resorting to chemicals. One or two layers of mulch placed over the soil can also reduce weeds as well as act as a barrier between the plants and diseases.

The benefits of an organic garden are many. It may take more time and more effort, but the hard work and results make it worth it. Organic gardening allows people to save money (and trips to the store) by eating their own homegrown vegetables. By eating organically grown food, one can avoid the many diseases caused by chemical exposure. Organic gardening also helps out Mother Nature by reducing waste and pollution as well as building healthier soil.

It is not difficult to have an organic garden. A person must simply be patient, adaptable and dedicated to giving back to the environment.

Chapter 13: Prairie Garden

A prairie is a low leveling temperate land which is predominantly covered by grass. In French it means "meadow". Prairies are common in North America and Canada. People have been attracted to the prairie gardens not just because of its beauty but also because prairie gardens need less maintenance compared to typical lawns.

The first thing to consider when creating a prairie garden is soil. Prairie gardens are low maintenance because the soil is naturally rich which ends the expense of fertilizers and pesticides. Prairie gardens also have a distinct unruly beauty because of its tall grasses which eliminates the weekly ritual of mowing your yard. An area of land that is level which gets full exposure to the sun is important because of the grasses and wildflowers you will want to grow. If converting a small space in your yard to a prairie garden start by sowing the seeds in containers because they grow faster than when directly planted. A lot of patience is needed when developing a prairie garden because perennial plants take a lot of time to bloom.

A Prairie garden is all about the different types and kinds of wildflowers you will want to plant. Wildflowers that are popular in prairie gardens are the Lance-leaf Coreopsis which is a yellow flower that grows in mid-summer and will give a refreshing atmosphere to your yard. Wild bergamot is a fragrant lavender flower that grows from mid-summer to early fall. If you want butterflies to add beauty to your garden, plant Meadow Blazingstars to attract them with their mauve purple flowers that bloom in late summer.

It may take a lot of patience and work in the first few years of creating and developing your prairie garden. Weed control is necessary as is keeping your plants trimmed and maintained. The big payoff to your patience and hard work is when your prairie garden's flowers bloom. Butterflies and birds are attracted to prairie gardens, as are friends, family and sometimes even neighbors.

Chapter 14: Raised Bed Garden

A raised garden is great for growing flowers, fruits or small vegetables. They are sometimes called garden boxes because they are contained in a wood structure. The advantages to a garden with a raised bed are as follows:

- Soil compaction is reduced which helps plants get the most air and moisture.
- With elevated beds, pathway weeds cannot find their way into your garden soil.
- The wood structure keeps your soil from eroding during heavy rains.
- Raised beds provide better drainage and less maintenance.
- Raised beds decrease the effort and difficulty of planting and harvesting.
- Crops can be planted ahead of season due to controlled soil conditions.

GARDEN STYLES

- With a raised bed garden poor soil conditions do not exist. Gardeners have total control on texture and soil ingredients.

Before starting a raised bed you will need to determine where to locate your garden and the size and shape of your bed(s). The area you put your raised garden should be flat, level, and have easy access to water sources. The depth of the bed will depend on which crops are going to be planted.

With minimal effort anyone can construct, plant and harvest in raised gardens. Both amateur and experienced gardeners will find raised bed gardens as overall timesavers.

CHAPTER 15: ROCK GARDEN

A Rock garden is a style that extensively uses rocks and stones along with plants and some accessories. It creates an impression of a dry garden because plants that are used in this style thrive very well in sandy soil and dry climate.

The rock garden is adopted by many garden enthusiasts, landscapers, and designers because the style suites most areas not just for its visual appeal but also for its function. For a small area, a rock garden can be arranged artistically to create a natural yet sprawling garden by having raised beds and layers made from rocks and stones. Similarly, if the area is a slope, the rock garden is perfect to support the soil yet adds appeal to the area.

A rock garden is a stunning and striking garden style because it allows for a unique color scheme. Additionally, naturally colored stone pieces and similar accessories can be arranged creatively to create personalized yet beautiful gardens.

GARDEN STYLES

The rock garden style requires little maintenance because its plant variety requires minimal care and easily thrives in any area whether it is exposed to the sun or in a shady area. Various plants in terms of height, form, and shape can be used in rock gardens to create a more interesting garden scene.

Most importantly, a rock garden can provide solutions for budget constraints because it uses natural resources such as rocks and stones. With just a little tweaking, these rocks and stones can turn out to look like expensive stone pieces.

Chapter 16: Rose Garden

With over one hundred species of this elegant flower it is important that a rose gardener is clear on what they want their garden to look like once the flowers are in bloom. Considerations like flower sizes, colors, height, and species should be noted and planned.

It is important for beginner rose gardeners to keep their first rose garden as simple as possible. Roses are highly sensitive plants and are often expensive, so the initial plant batch should include species that are easy to handle. It is always better to consult garden professionals regularly regarding the most adequate climate for different rose species, common types of rose diseases, and the best pest control methods available. Once armed with basic knowledge, preparation for the actual garden location can commence.

Roses love the sun and need at least six hours of sunlight exposure.

GARDEN STYLES

Morning sun is preferable as the afternoon sun may cause the flower and leaf colors to fade. Protection, like fences or hedges, can be placed strategically to control the sunlight received by the plants. However be aware that roses should be away from trees or structures that can cause water to drip down onto them. Too much water is not good for roses and especially water from the top of the plant. Roses will do their best with an exclusive watering system installed closer to the plant bed.

CHAPTER 17: SOUTHWEST GARDEN

To have a thriving garden in the Southwest, one must prepare for the climate. The Southwest includes Texas, Arizona, Southern New Mexico and most of the Mojave Desert. The heat of the summer months and the dry climate may seem daunting to some gardeners, but a garden in the Southwest is not impossible. In fact, anything that can grow in the Southern part of the United States, such as Magnolia trees and Hydrangea can still grow in a Southwest garden, provided there is enough water and healthy soil.

Southwest gardening is a form of desert gardening. Crops planted during late winter and spring flourishes better in Southwest gardens, as compared to the hot summer months. It is highly recommended to have raised beds while gardening. Raised beds ensure better soil. Vegetables planted in a desert garden should be irrigated weekly if the temperature is below 100 degrees and twice weekly if above 100 degrees. Sprinklers are inefficient for desert gardens due to the heat in the air. It is better to stick to drip irrigation. The location of the garden is also important. A shaded area is ideal, as the sun can be harsh on the plants during summer months.

Crops that grow well in the Southwest include peppers, tomatillos, tomatoes, lima beans, and onions. These vegetables grow fast and can be harvested quickly. It is also better to plant seedlings instead of seeds; the need for excess water after planting can be eliminated if seedlings are planted. Additionally, plants like peppers and tomatoes grow better in a shaded area. Mulching the soil after every harvest keeps the soil in the raised beds fertile. It also keeps the soil from drying up during the summer season. Overall, desert gardening is not that different from other types of gardening, once the climate and water situation have been overcome.

Chapter 18: Theme Garden

Having a central idea or topic that will serve as the basis of plants and landscaping is the basic definition of a theme garden. Garden themes can serve decorative or practical purposes depending on the interests and objectives of the garden owner. From the more formal to fun ideas, there are garden themes that can suit any land, climate, tastes and styles. Once the theme concept has been decided upon, the plants, materials, landscaping and other elements will fall into place.

The best thing about garden themes is that they are usually created around interests, hobbies or something else important to the garden enthusiast. For instance, people who are fascinated with the European culture create French or Italian-inspired gardens that have the laidback feel of the Mediterranean outdoors.

Theme gardens do not have to be inspired from a certain country or culture nor do they have to be practical in purpose such as a vegetable or herb garden. Anything that can be imagined and researched can be created.

Here are some themed ideas to get your creative juices flowing:

Alphabet Theme Garden – An alphabet garden is a fun and educational way to teach kids their ABC's. Find colorful and easy to grow plants for all 26 letters of the alphabet starting with azalea and ending with zinnias. Just be sure you have a large enough space to grow 26 plants.

Biblical Theme Garden – Garden contains plants mentioned in the Bible. Include the verse from the Bible that referred to the plant on a wooden sign beside each plant.

Color Theme Garden – Give any backyard a burst of beauty using a single shade of color to create a soothing, explosive, or unusual effect.

Music Theme Garden – Love music? Garden contains plants that have a musical reference. Plant suggestions include drumstick alliums, bugleweed, trumpet vine, coral-bells, and trumpet flower.

Pizza Theme Garden – Tomatoes, basil, rosemary, onions, peppers, garlic and oregano are toppings needed for a pizza. When it comes time to harvest your veggies, gather family and friends and have a home grown pizza party using your freshly picked toppings.

The possibilities for a theme garden are endless. Theme gardens can use a variety of herbs, vegetables, plants, flowers and other landscaping materials and you do not have to limit yourself to just one theme. Anything goes in a theme garden.

Chapter 19: Tropical Garden

With brightly colored flowers, plants with large leaves and lush scenery, it is easy to identify a tropical garden. This type of garden requires a generous amount of sunlight and rainfall which makes it more difficult to grow in colder surroundings. However, there are a variety of plants with bold colors that are hardy enough to survive the winter season yet still give off the impression of a tropical paradise.

In colder environments these gardens can be maintained inside a greenhouse. During the winter season it is common practice to take the plants indoors and put them back out during summer. Tropical gardens are typically dense and include plants with large leaves. To create a more effective tropical atmosphere, plants are huddled closer together. Ferns are the best example when it comes to providing great foliage. Narrow paths to create that jungle look are often found in these gardens and stone, gravel, wood and bamboo is commonly used as a detail for landscaping.

The usual trees found in a tropical garden are banana trees, citrus trees, plumeria, ficus plants and African tulip trees. The common tropical shrubs are hibiscus, jasmine, gardenia, bougainvillea, oleander and croton. The variety of colorful tropical flowers is one of the main reasons why people choose this garden theme. Orchids are a great choice but they require more care and maintenance compared to the other plants. Other exotic-looking flowers that easier to grow are lilies, begonias, petunias, African violets, gardenias and birds of paradise. Since not all of these can become readily available, some garden owners usually settle for native plants that have equally bright colors and still come up with the same tropical effect.

A tropical garden is one of the most difficult gardens to maintain and this is especially true in colder climates. With the right plants and enough creative arrangement it is possible to have a great tropical garden.

Chapter 20: Tuscan Garden

When you think of the word "Tuscan", the first thought that may come to mind is the contrast between elegance and peasantry lifestyle. Tuscany, the root of the word "Tuscan", is a region in Italy known for great wines, beautiful landscapes and home to great artists like Michelangelo, Leonardo da Vinci and Botecelli to name a few. Its people are regarded to be of high culture and their cooking is unique.

Tuscany was far from elegant in the earlier centuries due to being inhabited by farmers. Tuscany is known to be the birthplace of the Renaissance period and their garden designs have shown the power of that period. Though the gardens are grand, they are comfortable and romantic to behold. When trying to visualize a Tuscan garden think of Italian movies situated in the countryside showing farmers and their families gathered together in a backyard with fruit bearing trees, pots of herbs giving the air fragrance, a vegetable garden just within reach, and flowers beautifully arranged with vibrant colors.

To start your own Tuscan garden, evergreens can be planted to give your garden as they can give that Mediterranean look. This look is one component for that Tuscan feel. Hedges along the walkway, an Italian Cypress tree and olive trees are all parts of the design. Herbs like Sage, Thyme and Rosemary are important in a Tuscan garden because of the people's love for cooking. Lavender also adds a Tuscan atmosphere in your garden plus, beauty. Herbs can be planted in pots and then arranged decoratively in the garden. Herbs and vegetables make a Tuscan garden practical and iron works and a small fountain will complete the rustic, simple yet elegant Tuscan look.

The size of a Tuscan garden will depend on the gardener. It can be a whole backyard or just a small apartment patio. What is important when creating a Tuscan garden is the inviting atmosphere and the look of elegance with a romantic feel that can be enjoyed alone or with friends or family. A Tuscan garden is a simple yet beautiful and bountiful place where family and friends gather to celebrate and enjoy good conversation and good food.

Chapter 21: Vegetable Garden

The most basic explanation of a vegetable garden would be any garden that grows vegetables. A vegetable garden does not have to be big. This type of garden is a good way to guarantee a constant source of healthy vegetables right from the comforts of home. Growing vegetables is not a difficult task provided there is proper planning.

The first thing to consider is which crops to plant. There are vegetables that can produce only once, like carrots and radishes, while there are those that can be harvested multiple times, such as tomatoes and peppers. There are also climate and soil conditions to consider. Vegetable gardening is possible even in hot climates, as long as the plants are well taken care of.

There are three basic things any vegetable garden needs to thrive:

1. A location with plenty of direct sunlight that will provide six to eight hours of sun.

2. Ample water – A water supply or source must be near-by.

3. Good soil - Moist and well-drained soil mixed with organic matter is best for growing vegetables.

Maintaining your vegetable garden will require regular weeding. Mulching the soil is recommended to combat weeds and it can also modify soil temperature and conserve soil moisture. Constant watering is important to keep the vegetables growing. When harvest time comes, pick the ripened crops and reap the rewards of your vegetable garden!

Chapter 22: Vertical Garden

Vertical gardening is a method that trains plants to grow upward and off the ground instead of spreading out on the ground surface. Unlike conventional gardening methods, vertical gardens are ideal in populated urban areas where space and land is limited or non-existent. Vertical gardens are a popular option for apartment dwellers with balconies.

Vertical gardening reduces the area occupied by plants because they grow upwards and off of the ground. Fruits, vegetables and other plants are protected from damage because they are not in contact with the earth which reduces the use of pesticides. Reaping the rewards of your labor is easy because your plants are off the ground and hanging in plain sight.

GARDEN STYLES

Vertical Gardening is a method that eliminates all excuses for not having a garden and the design possibilities are only limited by one's surroundings, creativity or budget.

Chapter 23: Water Garden

Water gardens integrate architectural design with water features like fountains, ponds and waterfalls into a garden landscape. Aquatic gardens have been around since ancient times, and during those days, water was diverted from rivers and springs to create water features originally used for domestic fish production. This practice eventually evolved to more ornamental reasons, and the industrial age gave rise to modern pumps that are now being used to re-circulate the water in the garden.

Some types of aquatic gardens are fish ponds, stream gardens, water walls, reflecting pools and bog gardens. The construction of water features are typically small and shallow, as most aquatic plants can only thrive on depths of at least 20 inches. The depth and surface area of the pond is determined by the species of the plants and fishes which will ultimately thrive and create their own aquatic ecosystem. Besides the flora and fauna, other factors to be considered in the water garden are lighting, stone works, and statues that can blend in with the landscape.

GARDEN STYLES

There are mainly three types of plants used in a water garden:

1. Submerged
2. Marginal
3. Floating

Submerged plants are mostly underwater and only their leaves or flowers can be seen above the surface. These plants provide oxygen and nutrients to fish.

Marginal plants, otherwise known as emergent plants, have their roots underwater but the rest above the surface. Iris, cattails and lotus are considered to be marginal plants.

Floating plants, as the name suggests, are those that are free floating on the water's surface and are often used to provide shade and reduce algae growth in the water. The most common of these are water hyacinth and water lettuce.

Koi and goldfishes are the typical aquatic species found in garden ponds. As part of their maintenance, additional pumps and filtration systems are installed to keep oxygen in the water. In colder climates garden ponds have a small heater to prevent them from becoming frozen.

Chapter 24: Woodland Garden

A Woodland garden is a low-maintenance landscaping design where even a small space is adequate to create a garden that will stand out. The classic features of a woodland garden are trees growing near each other, making the area a forest of sorts.

It is important to know what kind of plants you should be planting in shaded or sunny areas of a woodland garden. Plants like the hosta plant, yew shrubs and periwinkle vinca are a few examples of plants that can grow in shaded areas under trees. For sunnier areas, low-growing plants like the yellow asylum are a good choice along with herbaceous plants. Also be sure to choose flowers that grow during each season so your garden will not be bare as each season begins and then passes.

While it is easy to keep a woodland garden in rural areas, it is harder to keep a woodland garden in the city with the restrictions of space and maintenance. In a city setting you can substitute the formality of a woodland garden by growing shrubs and evergreens in the space you have. For borders, instead of trees, hosta plants will create the same look of a forest while trapping the leaves from going to your neighbor's yard at the same time. As leaves fall, reuse them by shredding them and applying them to your plants as mulch, making the garden just as easy to maintain as the classic woodland garden.

Chapter 25: Zen Garden

The purpose of a Zen garden is to imitate the essence of nature. By delicately arranging rocks, water features, moss and pruned trees and bushes, and either gravel or sand that is often raked in such a way that imitates water ripples, Zen gardens create a peaceful environment. Often used for meditation, these Japanese gardens are beautiful places to better understand the true meaning of life apart from the business of the everyday world.

Perhaps the most important part of a Zen garden is the arrangement of the rocks. In the first known manual of Japanese garden, "creating a garden" is literally translated as "setting stones" or "act of setting stones upright." While traditional gardening is all about the flowers and the plants, the focus of a Zen garden is the rocks. Rocks can be used to create "mountains" or the borders of gravel "seashores" or "rivers" in the garden. Rocks that resemble animals or other unique shapes are often the main feature of the garden, a centerpiece of sorts. The rocks are rarely placed symmetrically or in lines. One of the more common assortments would be sets of three, or triads.

While sand is sometimes used, gravel is more common because sand is often disturbed by rain and wind. Raking gravel into "ripples" to resemble water creates a calming sensation. Creating perfect ripples requires a good deal of practice, so Zen priests often practice raking to improve their concentration.

One of the most unique aspects of a Zen garden is the mystique. You don't see everything at once. It takes time and concentration to notice the elements in a Zen garden, and this produces the meditation they are known for. Meditating can help deal with stress and several aspects of life in general.

Zen gardens are full of symbolism. From imitating landscapes to animals, they create a dreamy atmosphere. While very simple in appearance, the easiness on the eyes in no way indicates a lack of attention to detail. The smallest of details are perhaps what gives the gardens such a peaceful atmosphere. Whether a modern or ancient style, the minimalistic feel of Zen gardens is incredibly soothing. The literal interpretation of Zen is meditation, so these gardens are the perfect place to relax and refocus on truth and peace.

Chapter 26: Final Considerations In Selecting A Garden Style

With so many garden styles to choose from it is easy to become overwhelmed with options.

Here are some items to consider when selecting a garden style to suit your likes, needs and space.

Environment

Environment plays a lot in the success of gardening. It will determine the variety of plants that will thrive in your climate and geographical location. Also factor in local natural resources and conditions as well as the design of your home.

Soil Types

One of the most important considerations for selecting a garden style is determining the soil type. Certain plants need a specific type of soil in order to grow and be healthy. Most garden styles have specific groups of plants so your soil should determine the garden style that would be best suited for your area.

Purpose of the Area

You need to identify the purpose of the area because it will determine the suitable plants and accessories you are going to arrange. If the area is going to be a playground, then plants that have thorns should be avoided. On the other hand, if the garden area is close to your kitchen, planting herbs, fruits and vegetables would be ideal.

Maintenance

Do you like to spend time working in your garden or do you simply want to relax in it? Some garden styles require more work than others. Consider how much time and effort will be required to maintain the garden style selected.

Budget or Costs

If you are dreaming of a large exotic garden but budget is a constraint, then you might need to opt for a garden style that does not require expensive plants and accessories.

Personal Preferences

All that really matters when deciding on a garden style is to choose what is appealing to you and reflects your own personality. You, as the owner and gardener, will be the first person to admire the beauty of your garden.

MEET THE AUTHOR

Nina Greene grew up a country kid in the foothills of Northern California and acquired her love for the outdoors, gardening and landscaping from her father.

Forty plus years later, Nina still resides in NorCal and tends to her organic garden that provides fresh fruit, vegetables and herbs for family, friends, neighbors, co-workers and occasional wildlife.

Nina's "Gardening Basics for Beginners Series" is designed to help future garden enthusiasts get their hands dirty without feeling overwhelmed.

MORE BOOKS BY NINA GREENE

Gardening Basics for Beginners

Vertical Gardening: More Garden In Less Space

Milton Keynes UK
Ingram Content Group UK Ltd.
UKHW021449100624
443998UK00039B/784